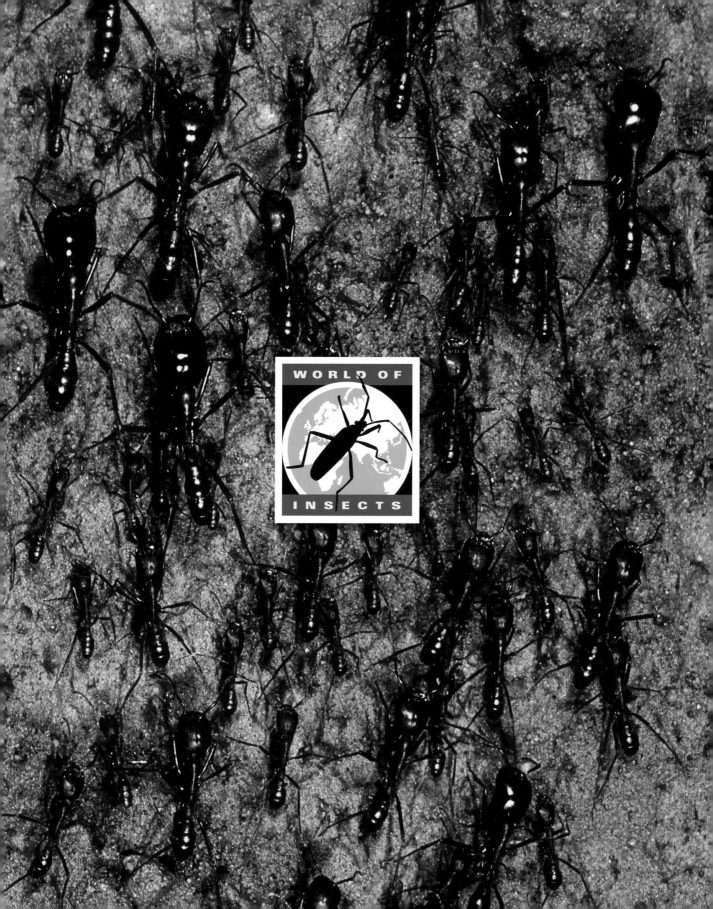

WORLD OF
INSECTS

ANTS

by Sophie Lockwood

*Content Adviser: Michael Breed, Ph.D., Professor,
Ecology and Evolutionary Biology,
The University of Colorado, Boulder*

THE CHILD'S WORLD®, MANKATO, MINNESOTA

Ants

Published in the United States of America by The Child's World®
1980 Lookout Drive • Mankato, MN 56003-1705
800-599-READ • www.childsworld.com

Acknowledgements:

The Child's World®: Mary Berendes, Publishing Director

The Creative Spark: Mary Francis, Project Director; Wendy Mead, Editor; Deborah Goodsite, Photo Researcher

The Design Lab: Kathleen Petelinsek, Designer, Production Artist, and Cartographer

Photos:

Cover: Zastavkin/iStockphoto.com; frontispiece and CIP: Martin Harvey/Corbis; half title: Zastavkin/iStockphoto.com.

Interior: Animals Animals/Earth Scenes: 5, 8 (J.A.L. Cooke/OSF), 18 (Fabio Colombini); iStockphoto.com: 11 (Roger Milego), 15 (Chartchai Meesangnin), 26 (Steve Simzer), 29 (Hung Meng Tan), 33 (Daniel Wrench); Minden Pictures: 9 (Christian Ziegler), 21, 24–25, 34 (Mark Moffett), 31 (Mitsuhiko Imamori); Oxford Scientific: 12 (Raymond Mendez), 16 (Bill Beatty), 30 (Patti Murray/Animals Animals/Earth Scenes); Photo Researchers, Inc.: 22 (J-P Varin/Jacana); Visuals Unlimited: 36–37 (Science VU/ARS).

Map: The Design Lab: 7.

Library of Congress Cataloging-in-Publication Data

Lockwood, Sophie.
  Ants / by Sophie Lockwood.
    p. cm.—(The world of insects)
  Includes index.
  ISBN-13: 978-1-59296-817-6 (library bound: alk. paper)
  ISBN-10: 1-59296-817-1 (library bound: alk. paper)
  1. Ants—Juvenile literature. I. Title.
  QL568.F7.L63 2007
  595.79'6—dc22   2006103452

TABLE OF CONTENTS

Chapter One

An Army of Ants

A group of army ants is on the move through the Amazon rainforest. It is nighttime, pitch dark, yet they slip over the undergrowth with remarkable ease. They march in a tidy column, 20 meters (66 feet) wide and 100 meters (328 feet) long. As they move, they collect their groceries— every beetle and bug, every spider and snake, every creepy, crawly critter in their way. These hungry **carnivores** have been known to eat lizards and even ground-nesting birds. Soldier ants efficiently dismember the prey they find and carry it along with the column.

The ants move silently, but their presence in the rainforest is never a secret. Ant thrushes and other birds perch in nearby trees, chattering to each other. Other creatures hear the warning cackle and pass it on. Hungry birds follow the column, picking up any creatures that may have escaped the river of foraging ants.

Army ants are hunter-gatherers, moving to a new **bivouac** site when the food supply runs low. They have existed in much the same way they are now for at least

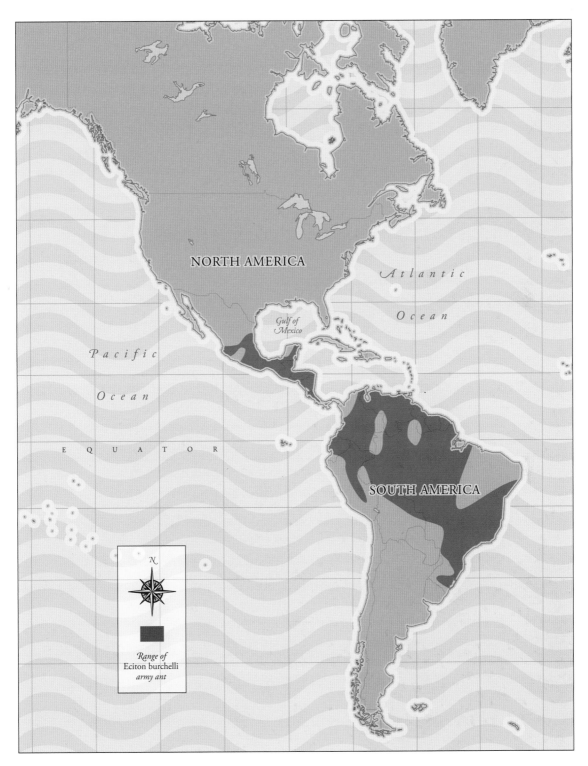

The Eciton burchelli *species of army ants can be found in Central and South America.*

100 million years. While other creatures have changed a lot over time, army ants have remained pretty much the same.

The army is made up of worker or soldier ants, a queen, and a few males. The workers are all **sterile** females. They cannot reproduce. Workers range from 3 millimeters to 12 millimeters (0.12 inches to 0.5 inches) long and live for several months. New workers in various stages of development continuously fill in the colony.

The queen is wingless. Her responsibility is to produce eggs—up to 4 million a month. It is the workers' duty to make sure she is well fed, protected from harm, and carried along with the colony. She

A queen army ant's body is filled with eggs.

Did You Know?
Army ants have no permanent home. When they arrive at their new temporary site, they build a living tent. Layer upon layer of linked, live ants form a dwelling to protect their queen.

rides in the center of the column atop a group of workers. She is too swollen with eggs to move on her own.

Males are only needed when a new queen is born or when the colony population grows too large and must split. Males are winged and live only long enough to mate with the queen. Within 48 hours of mating, a male army ant dies.

The army ant bivouac is extremely well organized. The queen is at the center, producing eggs. As new eggs arrive, workers move them around the center of the colony. The primary caretakers for the eggs, **larvae**, and

An army ant worker guards the colony's any larvae.

Would You Believe?
When hunting, the direction of the food raid changes an average of 123 degrees every day. The accuracy of the ants' navigating skills is amazing, especially since army ants are nearly blind.

pupae are called minims. Minims are smaller than soldier ants. As the larvae grow, minims move them farther from the center. The larvae spin cocoons as they advance into the pupae stage. New adults emerge and immediately go to work. They replace soldiers that have died off.

The army appears to have excellent time-keeping skills. Everything works according to a schedule. Once an area has been hunted out, the army ants go on the march for 17 days. Once it reaches its new stationary site, the army remains there for 15 days during which larvae grow. They have another stationary phase for 20 days during which the pupae develop. The stationary bivouac becomes like a headquarters for the army. Each morning at dawn scouts go out searching for food.

The colony remains in place for only a few weeks, until the queen has finished laying her new batch of eggs. Then scouts march out in search of a good hunting field. Once the new site is chosen, a ribbon of ants moves across the jungle floor again.

Chapter Two

The Ant Cycle of Life

Ants creep through the garden. They like to sneak into the kitchen and crawl on peanut butter sandwiches. They live in underground nests or in nests built in trees. They are social insects, much like wasps and some bees. They live in large groups whose individuals depend on each other for survival.

Ants can be found all around us.

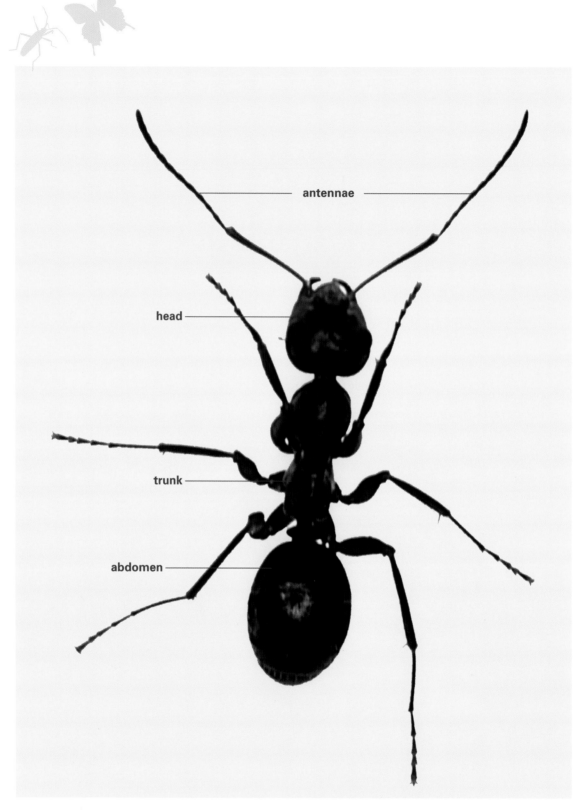

antennae

head

trunk

abdomen

The three main parts of an ant are the head, the trunk, and the abdomen.

As insects, all ant species have similar characteristics. They have jointed **antennae**. Workers do not have wings, and they live in colonies. Like other insects, ants have protective **exoskeletons** that surround their bodies. All ants have three body parts: a head, a trunk, and an abdomen.

An ant's head has eyes similar to those of flies. The eyes are multiple, tiny eyes connected together so the ant sees a broad range of activity. The two feelers, or antennae, are sensory organs that allow the ant to smell, touch, taste, and hear. Ants also have jaws, or mandibles, bearing pinchers that may deliver a nasty bite. Pinchers also allow ants to carry food.

The trunk includes all six legs. Each leg has a claw that enables the ant to climb up walls. The legs are also jointed with flexible, fringed ends.

The abdomen is an important part of an ant. In many ant species, it carries the poison sack and the stinger that allow ants to stun their prey or fend off **predators**. The stomach is also located in the abdomen.

Ants do not have the same internal organs as mammals. They have no lungs, but take in oxygen through tiny holes along their bodies that are called **spiracles**. Ants get rid of carbon dioxide through the same tiny holes. Blood is not pumped through blood vessels but through a long tube that runs the length of the body. Unlike human red blood, ant blood has no color.

Ants have no internal bones but an external skeleton, or shell, made of **chitin**, a substance found in both animals and plants. The ant nervous system is limited to a single nerve running the length of the body, much like the human spinal cord. Branches from this central nerve reach all parts of the ant body.

DEVELOPMENT

Ant reproduction depends on the queen. The queen lays millions of eggs in her lifetime, although not all survive to adulthood. The large number of eggs ensures that the colony will survive the many hazards that face ants: predators, floods, poison, and drought, for example.

Most of the eggs become female workers, which are much like the queen except they cannot lay eggs. The queen can lay male eggs and female eggs when the colony needs to split. Her body changes its chemical make-up to produce males. A chemical process occurs among the female worker eggs, allowing the females to become potential queens. Both the males and the females usually have wings. While most ant colonies have only one queen,

some species will support several queens, all reproducing at the same time.

Ant eggs quickly develop into larvae. These are help-less infants that rely on the workers to feed them. Larvae

An adult worker ant cares for eggs and younger ants.

go through several developmental stages called instars. An adult ant emerges from the final instar.

Adults also progress through several stages. They are like workers in a huge factory that begin doing entry-level jobs and are promoted throughout their lives. The new adult starts by caring for the queen and the young. The worker graduates to the more difficult task of digging and repairing the nest. An experienced worker moves on to search for food, followed by defending the nest. Since the lifespan of an adult ant is usually only a few months, an active nest must have thousands of workers in every stage of development.

New adult red ants look after the larvae.

Ants communicate with each other by touching their antennae and through chemical trails. The chemicals, called **pheromones**, provide a scent trail that other ants can follow. These pheromones are so powerful that 1 gram (0.04 ounces) of ant pheromone would be enough to make a trail that circles Earth.

Like bees and wasps, many ant species can deliver a power-packed sting. Some have chemicals that burn, while others can inject poison. True, it is very little poison from a very little defender. However, hundreds or thousands of such stings easily fend off an intruder. Most ants deliver their chemical warfare by means of a stinger, but some species can spray chemical substances in jets of fluid from their abdomens. The spray mechanism is much like a water pistol—only the substance sprayed is acid, not water.

Nature likes a comfortable balance of living things. There are billions upon billions of ants, and probably hundreds of predators that eat ants. In this way the immense ant population is kept under control. Ants are prey of spiders, ground beetles, and even other ant species. Among the ant-eating insects are antlions. Antlion larvae are serious predators. They build pits into which ants fall, and the antlions devour their visitors.

Did You Know?
Ants' closest relatives are bees and wasps. Ants are not related to termites other than both species are insects! Several ant species, such as matabele ants, regularly raid termite nests for food.

Insect-eating birds, such as woodpeckers and flickers, enjoy a tasty ant dinner, as do banded armadillos, five-lined skinks, and even bears. While a single ant doesn't seem like much of a meal for a bear, hungry bears have been known to dig up nests and devour ants by the thousands.

The best-known ant predators are ant-eating mammals: aardvarks of Africa, anteaters of South and Central America, and echidnas of Australia and New Guinea. These mammals have claws for breaking into nests and long, sticky tongues for capturing their share of an ant colony.

An anteater has found an ant nest and is having a snack.

Chapter Three

Ants, Ants, and More Ants

Ants have a long history. They evolved, or developed, from a type of wasplike insect from 168 to 140 million years ago. Winged ants today look remarkably like wasps. Scientists have found evidence of these early ant-wasp creatures sealed in amber and pressed between layers of sedimentary rock.

By 60 million years ago, ants had become dominant in many environments. They represented the largest amount of animal life in a given area. This situation continues today. Scientists think that ants represent about 15 percent of the **biomass** in an acre of tropical rainforest. Yes, they are small, weighing only fractions of a gram each. But, since there are probably 1 quadrillion—imagine billions of billions—living ants on the planet, that weight adds up.

Ants enjoy many different lifestyles. Some dig nests deep into the soil to set up housekeeping, while others prefer nests in the trees. Tiny wood ants found in Europe's Jura Mountains build huge pine-needle nests that can reach as high as 1.8 meters (5.9 feet). These ants create supercolonies with millions upon millions of ants. Dozens of nests in any one region are likely to be connected by underground tunnels, forming one massive colony. Weaver ants, on the other hand, build their nests from living tree leaves in the tropical forests of Africa and Asia. Weaver workers hold two leaves together, while other workers pass mature larvae back and forth to seal the edge of the nest. The larvae release a substance that is like sticky silk to hold the ants' leaf tent together.

Slavemaker ants are thieves. They rob eggs or larvae of other ant species from their nests. They raise the larvae to adulthood, and then turn the new workers into slaves. The slave ants labor willingly until they die. Amazon ants cannot feed themselves. They depend on slave workers stolen from other ant species to help them survive.

A number of ant species are vegetarians and actively farm fungi—a type of plant—deep in their nests. Leafcutter ants are among the farming species. They forage for plants in their area, dismantling a shrub with ease. Leafcutters do not eat the leaves, but chew them up to make **compost**.

They feed the compost to fungi—their primary source of nutrition. Leafcutter ants are just one of more than 200 fungus-farming ant species.

While army, driver, and siafu ants are carnivorous, most ants prefer a vegetarian lifestyle. Take harvester ants—gatherers who collect seeds. Much like

A leafcutter ant uses its pinchers and jaws to take out a piece of the plant.

Did You Know?
Ant troubles in your home? Try placing a hummingbird feeder filled with sugar water on the floor. The ants climb in and drown, and you won't need poison to kill them.

kangaroo rats, harvester ants store seeds to help them survive during periods of drought or bad weather. They build storage pantries within their nests, and use the reserve seeds only when no other food is available.

Strangely, at least one species of ant turns itself into a storage jar. Honeypot ant workers cannot move. Their

Honeypot ants can be found in many places, including the southwestern United States.

The Ant and the Acacia

On the African savanna, acacia trees flourish despite the greedy appetites of the environment's many plant eaters. One reason is that acacias stretch high enough so that only the tallest herbivores can reach their leaves. Another reason is the acacias' brutal thorns. Finally, acacias have developed a special relationship with stinging ants.

As an acacia grows, ants burrow into the tree's budding thorns. The thorns' centers provide good nutrition for the ants. In addition, acacias grow tiny buds that also feed their ant guests.

In return for food and a home, the ants protect the acacias from their worst enemy—giraffes. Acacia leaves are the giraffes' favorite food. The average giraffe measures 4.2 to 4.8 meters (13.8 to 15.8 feet) tall, the ideal height for finding acacia leaves. And, one giraffe eats about 30 kilograms (66 pounds) of leaves every day.

When the giraffe's long tongue yanks a bunch of leaves from an acacia, it shakes the branches. The shaking alerts the ants. They swarm to the source of the trouble and begin stinging the giraffe's tongue. A giraffe may only get two or three mouthfuls per tree before the stinging becomes too painful. Without the ants' protection, a giraffe might eat too many leaves and kill the tree. Thanks to the ants, giraffes get part of a meal, and acacias continue to thrive. The mutually helpful relationship between the ants and acacias is called **symbiosis**.

bodies store vast amounts of honeydew or nectar. The stores are used to feed other ants in their colony.

Honeydew is the **feces** of aphids and some caterpillars and is a much-prized feast for several species of ants. Black garden ant workers make sure there is plenty of honeydew for their colony—they farm aphids. This program works out well for the aphids, too. The ants protect the aphids from predators. The aphids eject honeydew to feed the ants.

There are so many species of ants, but there are several kinds that really stand out among the masses. Australia is home to bulldog ants with hideous pinchers that deliver a dreadful bite. Oddly, bulldog ants are vegetarians, but they hunt meat for their larvae. A bulldog ant can haul a grasshopper many times its own weight back to the nest with little trouble. Australia green ants are a nutritional snack that taste like lemon sherbet—tangy and sweet. Aborigines

A bulldog ant uses its pinchers on an insect.

grind them up and mix them in water to make a drink that tastes remarkably like lemonade.

Venomous ants can bother humans as well as other insects. In South America, bullet ants deliver a highly venomous sting. People in the southern United States constantly battle against fire ants, an aggressive species with a powerful sting. Humans turn aggressive whenever they see ants, too. When they see a parade of harmless carpenter ants across the kitchen floor, many people decide to bring out the heavy weapons—cans of bug spray.

Carpenter ants build their nests from wood fibers.

Chapter Four

In Appreciation of Ants

The Nez Perce, a Native American tribe of the Northwest, tell the legend of the Yellow Jacket and the Ant. Around campfires, the elders told their grandchildren this story:

The Chief of the Ants and the Chief of the Yellow Jackets were jealous of each other. Each wanted to maintain his rights but doing so was difficult.

Chief Yellow Jacket prepared to eat his favorite meal, dried salmon, on a certain rock. Chief Ant came by, furious at seeing Yellow Jacket upon the rock. "What right do you have to eat on that rock? You must have my permission to do so."

Chief Yellow Jacket laughed. "Ant, I always eat my dinner on this rock." Ant did not care. He felt Yellow Jacket was trespassing, and he would not give up his anger.

Ant and Yellow Jacket began to trade insults. Ant charged, and the two engaged in a fierce battle. Suddenly, a loud voice boomed, "Stop that fighting at once." It was Coyote. The battle did not stop.

Coyote yelled again, "Stop fighting immediately." Again the Ant and the Yellow Jacket ignored Coyote and kept fighting. They were locked together and too stubborn to give in.

Coyote warned, "You must stop fighting or I will turn you to stone." So, Coyote spun a magic spell and Ant and Yellow Jacket were turned to stone. They are there to this day, atop the rock they both claimed. Coyote understood the ways of the world—greed and a lust for power could bring down even great chiefs.

Many cultures passed down legends and tales about ants. Several Arab cultures admired the knowledge and ability of ants. They prayed that their children would develop the same characteristics as ants. To ensure this happening, parents put an ant in the hands of a newborn.

Some Native American groups put ants to a different use—as a torture for their captives. The prisoner was buried up to his neck in or near an anthill. Honey or some other sweet substance was poured over the prisoner's

head to attract the ants. The unfortunate prisoner was stung to death.

Ants are believed to have medical value. Soldier ants in the Amazon River basin have particularly strong bites. Warriors in the jungle used the soldier ants like stitches to draw open wounds

Did You Know?
In Aesop's fable, "The Ant and the Grasshopper," ants are admired for their work habits.

In some cultures, ants are admired for being hardworking.

together. The ant's head was placed against the cut. The ant bit down, and the ant's head was removed from its body. The jaws held fast, holding the flesh together until the cut healed.

Ants are also prized for their food value. Australian green ants not only taste lemony, they are also excellent sources of vitamin C. Ants are packed with protein,

Would You Believe?
Some people give credit to Saint Patrick for driving ants from the island of Puerto Rico.

Green ants are also known as weaver ants or green tree ants.

and both the ants and their larvae are eaten throughout the world. In fact, ants could easily provide a three-course meal, were you inclined eat them.

In Thailand, Khorat ant eggs and chopped flying ants make a delectable appetizer. Mexican gourmets dine happily on *escamoles,* ant larvae that have been roasted or sautéed—cooked in a little oil. Colombian natives favor *Colona* ants, toasted and popped in the mouth. Australian aborigines delight in the sweet treat provided by honeypot ants—an ideal dessert!

Considered a treat, a child eats a honeypot ant.

Chapter Five

Man and Ants

Humans have a mixed relationship with ants. We admire the ants for their work style, but we don't want them in our houses or our food. A trail of ants marching by carrying the food they scavenged fascinates us as long as they are not ruining our picnic.

Humans need to understand that ants provide valuable services in the natural world. They turn over the soil and distribute seeds. Ants also pollinate some fruit crops and plants. We need to understand that while Earth can survive well without humans, it would not survive without ants.

Ants fulfill an interesting role controlling pests. Third-century Chinese merchants sold ant nests to farmers to safeguard citrus trees. The ants warded off caterpillars and leaf-eating insects that might damage the flowers and reduce the production of fruit.

One of mankind's major problems with ants is dealing with alien ant species. Every continent has native ant species—ants that belong in Africa or South America or

Asia. Native ants have natural predators that keep the ant population under control. However, alien species are invaders. They can get a foothold in an environment and destroy the delicate balance of nature.

For example, cargo ships carried coffee and sugar from Argentina and Brazil to North America, Africa, and Europe in the early 1900s. The Argentine ant stowed away on those cargo ships, put ashore in a new environment, and created serious problems. In one

Did You Know?
How do alien ants arrive on foreign shores? They hitch a ride on ocean liners and cargo ships. All ocean liners have ant populations.

Usually thought of as pests, some ants actually help some crops and plants.

region, harvester ants were a native species. They buried seeds deep in their nest storage rooms. Argentine ants invaded and killed off the native harvester ants. So what?

Every few years, wildfires sweep across the savannas. Grasses, shrubs, and wildflowers die off. In the past, new plant life emerged when the rains came and seeds stored by harvester ants sprouted. Without harvester ants, the ecosystem and diversity of native plants changed. Invading ants destroyed the delicate balance of nature on African savannas.

Arriving in new locations on ocean-going ships, Argentine ants have caused environmental problems.

It is not just plants that suffer when ant invaders take hold. On remote Christmas Island in the South Pacific, yellow crazy ants arrived between 1915 and 1934. These ants formed multi-queen giant colonies that spread throughout the island. Crazy ants, so named because they run around aimlessly, killed off much of the island's crab population. Robber crabs, red crabs, and blue crabs were completely killed off.

The crabs were a **keystone species** on Christmas Island. Many other plants and animals depended on the existence of crabs for survival. Animals that preyed on the crabs went hungry. In some areas, crabs kept seedlings controlled by eating the sprouts. Weeds flourished without the crabs and invaded the forest. The entire ecosystem changed because the crabs no longer existed. And the crabs no longer existed because of yellow crazy ants.

Currently, the United States struggles under the rapid expansion of red imported fire ants. These ants arrived from Brazil, Argentina, or Paraguay about sixty years ago. Fire ant stings cause itching, blisters, and possible scarring. Pest control agencies have tried various poisons to kill fire ants, none of which has been particularly effective. Recently, the United States Department of Agriculture

Parts of the United States have been trying to stop the growth of fire ants.

began experimenting with phorid flies as a means of controlling fire ants. Phorid flies inject their eggs into fire ant soldiers. The ants die, and the fly maggots eat their way out of the bodies. They emerge as adults, mate, and begin injecting more eggs into more fire ants.

Conservation scientists have discovered that some ant species serve as **bioindicators**. They tell whether an environment is healthy or suffers from pollution. A habitat with no ants may have serious problems. Too many other animals and plants depend on ants. They eat them or feed them. These living things also share environments with ants. In a world that makes room for billions of people, there must also be space for those tiny, amazing insects—ants.

Glossary

antennae (an-TEH-nee) sensory organs that stick out of an animal's head

bioindicators (BI-oh-IHN-di-kay-turz) animals that show whether an ecosystem is healthy or polluted

biomass (BI-oh-mass) amount of living materials, such as plants and animals, in an area

bivouac (BIH-vuh-wak) a temporary camp

carnivores (KARN-nuh-vorz) meat eaters

chitin (KY-tin) a naturally forming substance found in animals and plants

compost (KAHM-pohst) decaying vegetable matter used to put nutrients back into the soil or to fertilize crops

conservation (kon-sur-VAY-shuhn) the act of saving or preserving some aspect of wildlife

exoskeletons (ECK-soh-skehl-eh-tunz) a hard outer shell found on animals such as lobsters and ants

feces (FEE-seez) the solid waste of animals

keystone species (KEE-stohn SPE-sheez) an animal or plant necessary for the survival of other living things in its environment

larva (LAHR-vuh) wormlike life stage of insects that develop into the pupa stage; the plural is _larvae_ (LARH-vee)

pheromones (FAIR-uh-mohnz) chemical substances made by an animal to attract mates or to create trails for others of the species to follow

predators (PRED-uh-turz) animals that hunt and kill other animals for food

pupa (PYOO-puh) the insect stage during which an immature larva develops into an adult; the plural is _pupae_ (PYOO-pee)

spiracles (SPEER-uh-kulz) small openings in the side of an insect that are used for breathing

sterile (STEH-ruhl) unable to produce young

symbiosis (sihm-by-OH-sis) a relationship between two living things that provides advantages to both

For More Information

Watch It

Ants and Plants, VHS. (Burbank, Calif.: Buena Vista Home Video, 1995.)

Nova: Ants, VHS. (Boston: WGBH Boston, 1995.)

Read It

Birch, Robin. *Ants Up Close.* Chicago: Raintree Publishing, 2004.

Fleisher, Paul. *Ants.* Tarrytown, NY: Benchmark Books, 2001.

Stone, Tanya. *Wild Wild World: Ants.* Farmington Hills, MI: Blackbirch Press, 2003.

Venn, Ceclia. *Ants and Other Social Insects.* Chicago: World Book Inc., 2000.

Look It Up

Visit our Web site for lots of links about ants:
http://www.childsworld.com/links

Note to Parents, Teachers, and Librarians: We routinely verify our Web links to make sure they are safe, active sites—so encourage your readers to check them out!

The Animal Kingdom
Where Do Ants Fit In?

Kingdom: Animal

Phylum: Arthropoda

Class: Insecta

Order: Hymenoptera

Species: 11,880 known species of ants

Location: Every continent except Antarctica

Index

About the Author

Sophie Lockwood is a former teacher and a longtime writer. She writes
textbooks, newspaper articles, and magazine articles. Sophie enjoys writing
about animals and their habits. The most interesting part of her research, Sophie
says, is learning how scientists apply their knowledge to save endangered
species. She lives with her husband in the foothills of the Blue Ridge Mountains.